# YOU ARE THE BEST!

# REAL LOVE

I
LOVE
YOU

XOXO

# CUTIE PIE

# CUP CAKE

FEBRUARY

# SWEET PEA

# YOU AND ME

# I LOVE YOU

# HUG ME

# ALL MINE

# BE TRUE

# SUN SHINE!

# ONE I LOVE

# YOU'RE SWEET

# Thank you for your recent purchase! We hope you've enjoyed your Valentine Coloring Card.
# Happy Valentine's Day!
# From florabella publishing

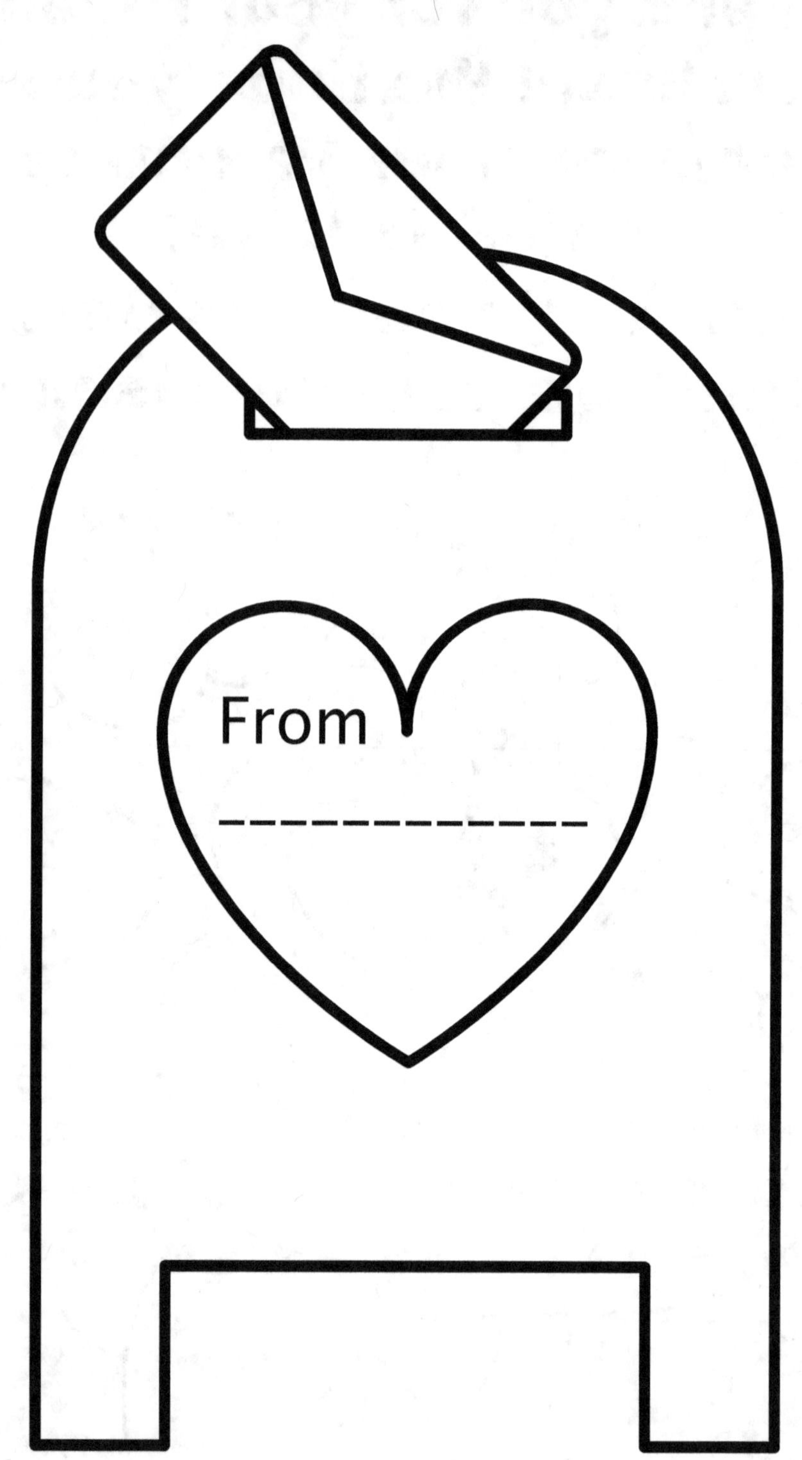

From